Copyright

Title book: WHAT SOCIAL MEDIA WILL TEACH YOU AND YOUR BUSINESS in 250 words or less

Author book: Kim Voller

For all the souls who pushed me beyond the edge.

Introduction

The vast arena of social media can give rise to many challenges along with opportunities. This book serves to inspire anyone and everyone who finds themselves using social media to grow not only their own personal brands but the brands of other companies and businesses. I guess you could say these are my personal journey notes through the world of social media. Every day I encounter a new lesson here, I see new ways of doing business and I can see how businesses are changing the way they work because of social media. There really is a mountain of knowledge in the social media realm; we all just need to learn how to organise it in a way that grows not only business needs, but also our own personal needs. It's a journey I hope all of you are enjoying and after reading this book, you will be able to continue to use social media to be better people and inspire others to be better versions of themselves.

Action (n)

The art of doing. Making things. Creating an answer to someone's question. Resolving issues. Sometimes movement is all that's needed by customers for them to trust you are doing something valuable. Don't stand still. You are not a tree.

Active Listening (v)

Ok. This concept technically shouldn't make sense. But if you tell people you are listening, they will trust you until they find that that's all you did. You need to listen, take note and then let your customer know you were listening. Give them an answer or work towards giving them some answers.

Adapt (v)

You cannot change your life overnight but you can change your direction in a moment. The road towards your objectives will constantly change so make sure you are aware and willing to change with it.

Allies (n)

People want to help you. if you are a part of social media you share a love of information and how that information is shared with thousands of others. You have knowledge and skills others could use, so get giving and others will give to you.

Alternatives (adj)

Go outside the box. We become old in our souls when we don't experience change. We stop discovering. We lose out on opportunity. I'm not saying that using alternatives will always work out but know that you have a chance to discover something great.

Anticipation (n)

I love a good Broadway show. The sense of anticipation and excitement is built up months before. Snippets of what's to come, flashes of costumes and characters are exposed. Your social media campaigns should follow this wisdom. Create a sense of something magic before you expose it.

Ask (v)

That little lesson your mother drilled into you
from an early age will always be valuable. Ask
and you shall receive. Ask and you will know. Only
by asking can you know your customer, your market
and even yourself.

Authenticity (n)

I fully support the statement "fake it till you
make it", but be authentic in doing it. Be open.
Customers want to be led by people. Real people. Not
a name or face or computer program but a human
being. The human experience is your greatest
selling weapon. Share your human experiences and
watch your credibility grow.

Awareness (n)

Humans demand the latest and greatest. People
want to be the first to experience the latest
trends, designs, fashions etc. Keep learning. Keep
up to date. Keep watching. Stay ahead of the trends
and give your clients access to this information.

Balance (n)

Stay balanced between your traffic volumes and your actual interactions. Yes. Drive your numbers with quality content, but make sure you are interacting with those people. You could have 20000 followers sitting in cyber space but are you actually giving them anything. Are they giving you anything? Is there any valuable interaction taking place. Balance your growth by driving both numbers and interactions.

Be Big (V)

Sometimes we are small. In our actions. In our thoughts. In our being. We surround ourselves with fear, doubt and maybe even a low self-esteem. We are so busy focusing on these fears and doubts, we don't recognise all that we really are. Believe in your power. Be BIG.

Being Noticed (v)

Get known. You are the key to your own success. Get liked. Genuinely. Inspire people to be interested in what you have to say. Be relevant and do stellar work. People will start looking and take notice.

Believe (v)

Visualise success. Know your value. You will only be as much as you think you are. Your customers and clients will believe the same. You cannot gain trust and value unless you know that you can give those traits to others.

Best Side (n)

Show off your best side. But don't deny your shadows. Inspire people by being a powerful personal brand. Build your own reflection and then build others. Become a force in the right circles and people will trust your credibility. Work at this everyday.

Bold (n)

If you have courage and you belief not only in yourself and what you can offer but also your concepts and ideas, you will be more successful in believing in the products and people you represent. Be bold in your approaches.

Brand (n)

Not only will you be representing brands created by others but you yourself will become a brand. Your skills, your online presence and your actions will define you. be relevant. Be credible. Be different from the rest. Become the brand people want to represent them.

Build (v)

Rome wasn't built in a day, neither was facebook. Take each action as a step towards the bigger picture and be patient with your goals. Remember to build on your successes, don't waste them. boast about it. let people know you know what you are doing. Once you have built one house, you can build an empire.

Champions (n)

Some people know their *shizz*. They are talented and know their influence. They use it wisely. They believe in themselves, their work and their clients. These people can teach you something, even if you just observe their processes. Seek them out. If you are really lucky they will be able to offer you some valuable wisdom. Take it with both hands.

Change (v)

The ability to adapt. The way forward is never really straightforward. Be an agent of change. Business is rarely standing still. Your clients WILL change. They will change their minds, change their products, and change their budgets. Be flexible and ready.

Chat (v)

Communication is customer gold. This includes listening, responding, advising, apologizing, changing and moving forward.

Collaboration (n)

"Seek those who fan your flames." Rumi

Just remember strength in numbers. Use each other to get further. Some people have skills you may just not have, and the same goes for you. Together we can get a lot more done and done smarter. Build your connections.

Comfort Zone (n)

In the realm of social media, there is no comfort zone. Every possibility, every avenue is a chance to be something new. A chance to think out of the box. We don't work in a comfort zone. Ever.

Community (n)

Social media networks are some of the greatest communities ever built. You will soon realise the value in them. Here is my advice: Go where the people are. Stand in the middle of that crowd. Introduce yourself. Keep talking. Soon the word will spread. Soon you become friends. Stay connected.

Competition (n)

We all want to be at the top. But just remember that sometimes, being 2nd without a view of the finish line, gives you a chance to see a better, faster, efficient way to the top. Being in front is not always the most successful.

Consistency (n)

If you learn anything, let it be this. CONSISTENCY.
Act and react in the same way as you always do.
Just make sure its effective. Don't rock the boat if
you are smooth sailing. Never ever become silent or
unresponsive. People hate silence, especially if it
is what you do. Acknowledge them and then figure
out a game plan. Be consistent always.

Content (n)

This topic is vast. But let's summarise the
fundamental rule of content. Always ask yourself
"why does this matter?" Have a look at the "needs"
you are driving to meet. Find ways of meeting these
needs with creative content. Keep your content
relevant, consistent and innovative. Change it up,
use different platforms, media or ways of showing
off your content. Let this content then drive your
connections.

Conversation (n)

Best had two ways ←--------→

Create (v)

Every time you start something, you are creating something into being. This is no ordinary process. You are adding to the fibre of the universe. Be the cause of creation.

Develop (v)

A decision to think differently can be the difference between fall or fly. Keep finding new ways of doing things.

Direction (n)

It will most defiantly change. A lot. Be in sync with your clients and your customers. You need to know that where they want to go is not always where you are headed. Lead, don't follow.

Distraction (n)

Don't be driven by lists, fans, followers or likes. These things are ego boosters. Sure it feels good and may give a sense of credibility but don't get distracted by the relevance of those contributors. You need to stay focused on valuable audience engagement. People wanting to interact with you, and you providing that service. That should make you feel good.

Do good (v)

Think before you act. Listen than respond. Keep evolving and stay positive. People and companies like good people. Be good.

Do-er (adj)

Don't wait. Ever. Just don't. there is never a right time. The conditions will never be most favourable. Trust yourself to make the right decisions and get things done. Persevere.

Dreams (n)

If you don't have any, find some. Grow them. They too will change with you. Nurture the dreams of others. Your clients, companies and your audience may need you. Your contribution can grow dreams or destroy them. So be aware.

Emotion (n)

Emotion drives people. People want their emotional needs met. This is essentially how people grow. A product satisfies a need. Engage with your clients and establish which need their product is satisfying and then continually work to fulfil it.

Engage (v)

The more you engage, the more value you find in yourself and the more others will find value in you.

Evaluate (v)

Continuously. Track your progress. Measure your success and your failures. Analysis how to make the necessary changes to improve. You will need to know if your master plans are working.

Exception (n)

Be the best at who you are and you will be the best at what you do. Don't follow the norm, it truly is very boring…

Failure (n)

LEARN FROM IT. ITS GOING TO HAPPEN. HOPEFULLY NOT
THE SAME WAY TWICE.

Fine tune (v)

You can't have it all. Some ideas, concept and
opportunities are meant to be let go. Fine tune
your plans and stay focused until they are
complete. More will come your way I promise.

Flow (n)

If it feels good and it has flow then trust that
this is where you need to go. Dream the journey,
live the dream. Keep going.

Focus (v)

Focus on what your clients and their customers
are saying and then do something about it. If you
can't change it, focus on finding some smashing
alternatives.

Give & Take

A fine art can be made by what you give and take in the exact proportions needed to make your life more than what it was yesterday. Same goes for business. Spend time learning this art.

Great (adj)

Get used to great. You are great. Even by just being in the world, you are being great. Now make a choice. Are you going to be great today? Don't worry about the how.., it starts with the choice to contribute to the greatness you already are.

Gumption (n)

Use what you have, where you are, knowing your limits and get the job done. Challenges need courage to overcome. Grow your gumption.

Habit (n)

Create healthy habits that work for you. and your business. Consistent actions that make you feel good. Habits will keep you going when times get tough. Let people identify you by your fabulous habits.

High 5 (v)

Always return the high 5 to the companies and individuals who recognise and acknowledge your awesome talents. Affirmation grows people. Let's be honest, who doesn't love a good old high 5!!

Identity (n)

You are your business. You are what you reflect out into the big bad world. Ultimately when people identify your business, they will identify you. So be the mirror. Happy successful YOU = Happy successful BUSINESS.

Intuition (n)

If you feel it, believe it. Intuition always plays a part. Trust your gut. Your customers will also use theirs. So make sure you are sending out good vibes.

Influence (n)

Your actions will always speak volumes more than any thought you can muster. You don't sell products; you sell your client, their attitudes and their values. Brand them with influential excellence!

Innovation (n)

Peter Drucker says that business enterprises have two basic functions. Marketing and Innovation. They produce results, all the rest are just costs. So make sure your social media enterprises revolve around creation and that you are constantly innovating greatness.

Inspire (v)

Everyone you know or meet knows something you don't. Including yourself. Inspire everyone to be better. Talent lies in changing others to become better. And be open to letting others inspire you.

Intention (n)

Be deliberate in your actions.

Integration (n)

It's not about what's easy, or which social media platform you prefer. It shouldn't even be about the money, although this can be a factor. Its about combining the simplest, cheapest, yet most efficient system or series of systems to increase your brands influence. Connections made quickly, easily and effectively is the goal.

Keep Going (v)

They say adventure is conquering your fears. I say to choose to get out of bed every morning and face your daily taskls is the bravest start to any adventure. Keep going!

Leadership (n)

You will make mistakes. But it truly comes down to what you do with them that counts. Being able to alter circumstances favourably and inspire others to do the same is how you should lead.

Lurker (n)

90% of people on your social media platforms are considered lurkers. Your goal should always be to change these unresponsive potential contributors into engaging and responsive information sources.

Mobile (n)

At every opportunity push mobile. Push the use of this technology in your personal life and your business. It's the way of the future. Make your customers aware of the possibility here.

Needs (n)

In the end business is about meeting a need. Humans need their needs met in order to grow. Business people need to hook onto these needs and fulfil them. Social media is an excellent tool to help you do this, by solving problems, make a customer feel valued or even just a freebie. Keep identifying the needs and consistently meet them.

Never Sleeps

Your brand never sleeps. There is always someone watching. Simple. Don't switch off. Schedule your work. Be available.

Notice (v)

Take note of everything. Every time. Don't slack on this. You will need to be aware at all times. Social media changes faster than you can blink. If you lag behind, you miss opportunity and will be become irrelevant to your customers. Someone else will grab your moment.

Own it (v)

Value your footprint on the world. Your ideas and your impact are worth something to someone. You were big and bold enough to create them so own it, and everything that comes with it.

Participation (n)

You offer a service. But that doesn't mean you sit back and become a witness to events that unfold from offering that service. Get involved. Stay involved. The only way to know what is relevant is to stay in the thick of it. Don't become that silent mysterious type. It may be attractive in a Spanish action film but in social media it's probably the worst thing you could do.

Pay Attention (v)

ALL THE TIME

Persistence (n)

Everyday we build, we break, we fall, we recover, we step back, we move forward. The point is we are always moving. Don't give up.

Personal Brand (n)

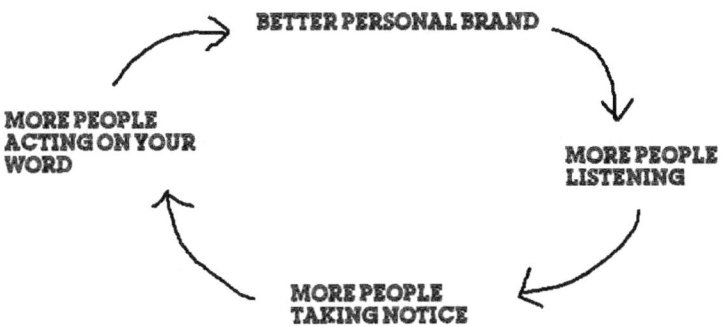

Presence (n)

Every time you put something out there into the universe you have a chance of it being seen, being heard, taken in, copied, acted upon or shared. Think wisely.

Protect (v)

Be involved in the protection of brands you represent, if your own, even more so. Protect their identity and most of all their reputation. Stand up against mis-use of your brands identity.

Purpose (n)

You need to act with clarity everyday so that your actions catch up with your vision. Be driven to produce excellence.

Relationships (n)

It's a fine art, this relationship business. We need to constantly nurture them, create new ones and be brave enough to leave ones that no longer serve us. It's a lot like life this social media game.

Relevance (n)

It makes no sense to use language that interested people won't understand. Don't be "bitchin & bangin" when talking about dental care. Be relevant and engage with clarity.

Research (n)

DON'T STOP LEARNING

Resolution (n)

Embrace the bad or negative aspects of your efforts. Be open about it. then make a concerted effort to change it. There may be resistance but eventually if you persist you will find a way to resolve uncertainty. Your customers and connections will be open to your efforts.

Schedule (v)

Life happens in real time. Things are unpredictable. We cant plan and schedule everything, even if we wanted to. You can organise information but be open to allowing for unforeseen events and actions which could change your game plan. Eye's open!

Shadows (n)

There will be dark days. You will make mistakes. You will need to grovel and apologise and correct your mistakes. Maybe even other peoples mistakes too. Don't deny your shadows. We are all human and we make mistakes. Your customers will appreciate your humanness.

Show off (v)

If you do this right you will do nothing but
inspire change. Show off your talents, your
knowledge and your good habits. Help people who
need you, by showing them what you can do. You are
amazing. Sell yourself.

Silence (n)

Even your silence can be the most powerful impact
you make. Use it wisely.

Size (n)

It only matters for some things......

Engagement over numbers is the key here. Talk to
people. Make connections. Its great to have many
connections but you get nothing from that
connection unless you engage in some interaction.
Make sure the impact is always greater than the
numbers.

Strategy (n)

Let me share my simple strategy for all my social media interactions. These range from paying clients to people looking for advice, to my own interactions. I strive to practice this process continually because I know it leads to success in social media.

1st = See

2nd = Follow

3rd = Act

4th = Change

Success (n)

Success breeds success. If you realize that it depends on nothing you have done in the past. You need to work as if there was no success.

Tangible (n)

It's often hard to trust something you can't see or measure. People tend to be sceptical over concepts and ideas with no form. Social media can be tricky. Tricky to measure its impact and to see the influence on the bottom line. All you need to know is social media interactions and even mere presence can influence and contribute to your bottom line. There is plenty of research out there to support this. Your efforts online will become tangible in your business's bottom line earnings.

Time (n)

Time is just an excuse. Think in ideas, concepts and revolutions. You either complete them or you don't. Time is just an excuse.

Transparency (n)

A fundamental business practise. If you don't hold this to the core of your business dealings, you will always struggle to hold valuable connections with others. There will always be a secret, or a hidden piece of information which could impact others. I wouldn't want to do business with a company like that, would you?

Trust (v)

Trust is earned. Dependable actions and a proven track record creates loyalty. Don't promise or compromise. Just be consistent in your interactions. Create a trustful environment and relationships with people.

Unique (n)

BE UNIQUE IN YOUR APPROACH. LEAD, DON'T FOLLOW.

Value (v)

Value = Brand power. With power comes responsibility. Use your value wisely. Change the world with who you are. Set yourself on fire.

Viral (n)

You have to get your information moving. Think of a cold passing amongst 5 year olds. It needs to move quickly between people. Set your information on fire.

Weeds (n)

We need to be like weeds. Have the uncanny ability to grow from nothing, in the most unlikely places and endure the harshest conditions. Be admirable.